MERCURY

ROBERT DAILY

MERCURY

A FIRST BOOK
FRANKLIN WATTS
NEW YORK/CHICAGO/LONDON/TORONTO/SYDNEY

To My Parents

Cover photograph copyright © NASA
Photographs copyright ©: Finley Holiday Films: p. 8; North Wind
Picture Archives: p. 13; Stock Montage/Historical Pictures Service:
pp. 15, 17, 36; NASA: pp. 21, 24, 31, 34, 39, 52, 55; ROE/ATT
Board: p. 27; Don Dixon Spacescapes: pp. 29, 42, 49; Hansen
Planetarium: p. 46; Peter Rosenbaum, 1993: p 64.

Library of Congress Cataloging-in-Publication Data

Daily, Robert.
    Mercury / by Robert Daily.
      p. cm. — (First book)
    Includes bibliographical references and index.
    ISBN 0-531-20164-3
      1. Mercury (Planet) — Juvenile literature. [1. Mercury
(Planet)] I. Series
QB611.D35 1994
523.4'1—dc20   93-6100   CIP   AC

CONTENTS

MYSTERIOUS MERCURY

CHAPTER ONE

On the afternoon of March 29, 1974, in a California basement, nervous scientists huddled around a television screen — not to watch a soap opera or a ball game, but to witness the very first pictures from a faraway world. More than 91 million miles (147 million km) away, the planet Mercury was getting its first visitor from Earth. Traveling at a speed of 7 miles (11 km) per second, a spacecraft named *Mariner 10* zipped past the planet's surface.

Mariner 10 looked like an oversize space-age bug, with a pair of solar panels (each nearly 10 feet [3 m] long) for "wings," and all sorts of antennas sticking out. One of those arms held a video camera. It flashed its pic-

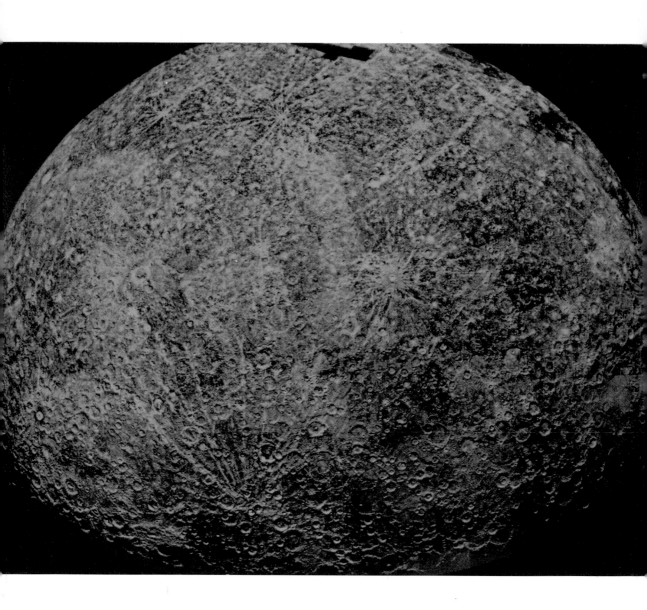

Photographs such as this one from Mariner 10 gave scientists their first look at Mercury's scarred and wrinkled face.

tures to a giant antenna in the Mojave Desert in southeast California. Those signals were then relayed to the Mission Control Room in the Jet Propulsion Laboratory, in the San Gabriel Mountains north of Los Angeles.

As the pictures flashed on the television monitors, the scientists saw images of a mysterious landscape. After forever hiding from our view in the sun's glare, Mercury was finally showing its scarred, wrinkled face.

PLANET OF EXTREMES

Mercury has always been a mystery planet, mostly because it is very hard to see. Mercury is the sun's closest planetary neighbor, and the glare from the sun, combined with the thick, polluted *atmosphere* surrounding Earth, makes it one of the most difficult planets to spot. Also, Mercury never appears high in Earth's sky, where planets are best seen. It is almost never seen at night, and those rare times when it does appear at night are only just after sunset or just before sunrise, when it is close to the horizon. Trying to view it through a telescope can be very frustrating.

Another reason for Mercury's mystery is that *astronomers* have concentrated on other planets. Venus and Mars, our closest neighbors, have each been visited by a dozen or so spacecraft. Mercury has been visited only once, by *Mariner 10*, and only one side of the planet has been photographed. But the *Mariner 10* expedition taught us a lot about Mercury. It revealed a fascinating world similar to the Earth's moon in several ways. A world that at one time used to gurgle with volcanic activity; a world where mile-high cliffs cut across the surface; a world of enormous holes created by *meteoroids* smashing into its surface.

Mercury is a world of superlatives and extremes. It is the quickest planet, traveling through space as fast as 128,000 miles (206,000 km) per hour. If an airplane could fly at that speed it could circle Earth in less than twelve minutes.

Mercury is, after Pluto, the smallest planet. It would take almost eighteen Mercurys to fill our own Earth. Mercury is also (if you allow for the squeezing effects of *gravity*) the densest planet. That means its materials are the most tightly packed together. Finally, Mercury has the smallest *orbit*, because it is the closest planet to the sun. And, though it is not quite as hot as Venus (the second closest), no other planet has such a wide temperature range. The parts of Mercury's surface that experience daylight are as hot as blazes, baked in temperatures hot enough to melt lead. The other parts that undergo night are cold enough to be covered with vast sheets of ice.

ANCIENT BELIEFS

Mercury was probably noticed by prehistoric people. In fact, it might have been easier to spot Mercury back then, before cars and factories polluted Earth's atmosphere and before bright lights made it harder to see objects in the night sky.

In the past, the planets were an important part of religious life and were named after gods. So, throughout the ages, the planet we call Mercury has had many names. The Egyptians named it Sobkou. It was known as Bi-ib-bon to the Sumerians; the Assyrians called it Goudond. The Chaldeans, who also called it Goudond, drew pictures of the planet in a robe and tiara — like a king or a queen.

They also gave it wings to explain its rapid motion.

The Babylonians called it Nabou, the Ruler of the Universe. He was the only one who could wake the sun from its bed and make it move across the sky. The early Scandinavians named the planet Odin, after the father of the gods. The ancient Germanic people called it Woden. They named the middle day of the week after the planet — Woden's day, or Wednesday.

The Greeks had a god named Hermes who carried messages for the other gods because he had wings and could move very fast. When the Greeks discovered a fast-moving planet, they named it for Hermes. Actually, they thought Mercury was two different planets, one that appeared in the morning, the other at night. This night planet, they called Hermes; the morning one they named Apollo, after the god of the sun. The Romans kept many of the Greek gods but changed their names. So Hermes became Mercury.

Before the telescope was invented, the planet's name was almost all that people knew for certain about Mercury. In the 1500s, a Polish astronomer named Nicolaus Copernicus

To ancient Romans, Mercury was the
messenger god, a winged creature who
could travel very fast. Therefore, they
gave the fastest planet his name.

(1473–1543) revived an ancient Greek idea that the sun is at the center of the solar system and that all the planets revolve around it. Although Copernicus was correct, few people believed him for nearly a century. He also correctly placed Mercury as the sun's closest neighbor.

Copernicus calculated that a year on Mercury lasted about eighty-eight Earth days. (An Earth year is 365 days, more than four times as long.) In other words, it takes eighty-eight days for Mercury to orbit the sun. This is the shortest year of any of the planets. Mercury is not only the fastest-moving planet but also the closest one to the sun and therefore has the shortest path (or orbit) to travel.

THROUGH THE LOOKING GLASS

When the telescope was first used to look at the heavens in 1609, astronomers started learning more about Mercury, even though the sun's closest neighbor was the hardest planet to spot.

The Italian astronomer and physicist Galileo Galilei (1564–1642) wanted to prove that Mercury goes through phases. As this inner-

The Italian astronomer Galileo Galilei, shown here in Venice, tried to prove that Mercury goes through phases. Unfortunately, his telescope was too weak to see the planet very clearly.

most planet circled the sun, Galileo supposed, different amounts of its sunlit side (or day side) would face Earth, as the angle between Earth, the sun, and Mercury changed. Galileo observed that Venus goes through phases that are far easier to see than those of Mercury. (Earth's moon also shows phases.) His telescope was too weak, however, to give him a good look at Mercury.

In 1639, an Italian named Giovanni Zupus used a more powerful telescope to prove his countryman correct: Mercury does indeed go through phases. (This evidence also proved Copernicus's theory. A planet closer to the sun than Earth could show a full cycle of phases only if it orbited the sun, not Earth.)

In the 1700s, still more powerful telescopes helped astronomers measure Mercury's diameter. Their estimates ranged from 2,700 to 4,000 miles (4,350 to 6,440 km). Among the known planets in the solar system, Mercury was the smallest. In 1980, Pluto was measured at a diameter between 1,800 and 2,200 miles (2,900 and 3,540 km), making it the smallest.

Mercury was so small that early astronomers were frustrated when they tried to draw maps of its surface. And the scientists who tried to measure its rate of rotation — the time it takes to spin once around its own axis — were really frustrated. These scientists also needed surface markings; by tracking them they could figure out how long Mercury took to spin. In Italy, Giovanni V. Schiaparelli (1835–1910) observed Mercury from 1882 to 1889. Because he could barely see the surface

Giovanni Schiaparelli measured Mercury's rotation by keeping track of surface markings as the planet spun.

markings and thought they didn't move, he concluded that Mercury rotated once every eighty-eight days, the same number of days it took for the planet to orbit the sun.

If Schiaparelli had been right (and scientists believed he was right until just a few decades ago), then one side of Mercury was always facing the sun, and thus very hot. The other side was always dark and always very cold.

MODERN DISCOVERIES

Giant telescopes were built by the 1900s, but even these powerful instruments could not tell us what we needed to know about the sun's neighbor. Mars had been fairly well mapped, but Mercury's surface was only vaguely chart-ed. In fact, books published as late as the 1970s continued to contain incorrect informa-tion about Mercury.

During World War II, scientists developed a technique called *radar* (for *radio detection and ranging*), which taught them a good deal about Mercury. Radar works by bouncing radio waves off a moving object. Scientists compare the frequency of the returning waves with the ones that were transmitted and can determine how fast the object is moving. Today police use radar the same way to catch motorists who speed.

In 1965, American scientists, using a radio telescope that could also serve as a radar dish in Puerto Rico, learned that Mercury was spinning faster than had been imagined. Today, we know that Mercury's rotation period is 58.6 days long.

Later radar experiments measured Mercury's diameter to a more precise degree, estimated the planet's *mass* (the amount of matter), and made guesses about the roughness of its surface.

Yet our knowledge of Mercury, compared to our knowledge of Mars and the moon, remained quite small. In some ways, we didn't know much more about Mercury than did Copernicus or Galileo. There were so many unanswered questions: Was Mercury rough and craggy like the moon, or smooth like a billiard ball? Did it have an atmosphere? How about a *magnetic field*? Would we find any signs of life, past or present?

It would be up to the flying bug named *Mariner 10* to answer these questions.

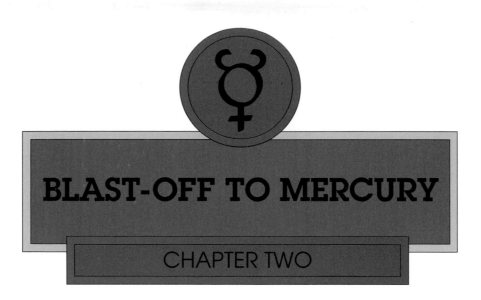

BLAST-OFF TO MERCURY

CHAPTER TWO

The space age kicked into gear in October 1957, when the Soviet Union launched the first artificial satellite. A month later, a Russian dog named Laika became the first astropup; the first human cosmonaut followed in 1961. The first human on the moon, American astronaut Neil Armstrong, landed there in 1969.

Mercury was too far away — and too hot or too cold, depending on which side you visited — for a manned landing. Instead, scientists dreamed of sending a spacecraft called a *probe*, which carries cameras and scientific instruments but no people. A probe never returns to Earth but relays its pictures and information back to Earth by radio waves.

Top: The Soviet Union's first artificial satellite, Sputnik, kicked off the space age. Bottom: An early probe. This one, Mariner E, traveled to Mercury's neighbor Venus in 1967.

Probes had already visited Venus (in 1962 and 1967), Mars (in 1964, 1969, and 1971), and Jupiter (in 1972), but never Mercury. Finally, the U.S. Congress approved money for a mission, called *Mariner 10*, that would blast off in 1973.

The mission team decided that the *Mariner 10* spacecraft would visit two planets in one trip, passing by Venus on its way to Mercury. That way scientists could learn more about Venus, Earth's nearest planetary neighbor. More important, the spaceship could use the *gravitational field* of Venus to change directions without large amounts of fuel. Valuable space that would otherwise have been needed for fuel could then be used to carry more scientific instruments.

Such a technique, called a "gravity-assist trajectory," was not an easy thing to plan. According to scientist Robert Strom it was as hard as "hitting a dime with a bullet fired from a distance of about 12 kilometers [7 miles]." The two planets were in the proper locations in relation to each other for only a short time. If *Mariner 10* missed in 1973, scientists would have to wait another decade for a similar positioning of the planets.

The mission presented another problem: a spacecraft had never passed so close to the sun. The sun was a friend, because it would provide energy to the probe through two solar panels. But it was also an enemy: scientists had to surround *Mariner 10* with sun shades and thermal blankets to protect the sensitive instruments from the intense heat.

The solar panels looked like wings sticking out from the eight-sided main structure. They could be tilted to maintain the proper temperature. *Mariner 10* also carried gas jets for stabilization and control, a rocket to adjust the path, and two antennas. Two video cameras were attached to a telescope that could make a newspaper readable from a quarter of a mile (0.4 km) away.

Mariner 10 blasted off from Cape Canaveral, Florida, on November 3, 1973. Immediately it ran into trouble. Changes in temperature caused a drain on the power system, and also cracked an antenna. Scientists on the ground, however, were able to fix these problems by remote control.

The spaceship raced past Venus on February 5, 1974, taking thousands of pictures. On March 29, it reached Mercury, the first spacecraft to do so, and continued moving on.

A drawing of Mariner 10, showing its flight path as it
blasts off from Earth, skims past Venus, and heads
toward its ultimate destination, Mercury.

On its first flyby, *Mariner 10* took pictures of the planet's two half-lit sides. It orbited the sun and met up with Mercury again on September 21, passing the "day," or sunlit, side. The pictures taken on this second pass linked the two sides that were imaged on the first trip. Its orbit around the sun allowed *Mariner 10* to make a third visit on March 16, 1975, taking photographs of the "night" side. The probe passed within 204 miles (327 km) of Mercury's surface, the closest a spaceship has ever gotten to any planet other than Earth.

Mariner 10's voyage within the inner solar system was a great success. Traveling more than 1 billion miles (1.6 billion km) in 506 days, this flying laboratory made thousands of measurements and took thousands of pictures. All told, it photographed nearly half the planet's surface.

Almost all of what we know today about Mercury comes from this mission. In fact, we discovered more in a single year than we had learned in all the centuries before.

Although we have lost contact with the spacecraft, it continues to endlessly circle the sun. Every 176 days it passes Mercury, the planet that would still be a mystery if not for *Mariner 10*.

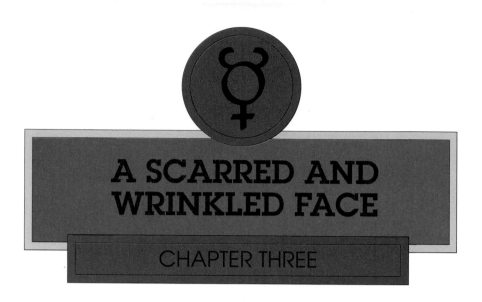

A SCARRED AND WRINKLED FACE

CHAPTER THREE

Mariner 10 gave scientists their first up-close and detailed glimpse of Mercury's surface features. At first glance, the pictures that *Mariner 10* sent back show a planet that looks a lot like our moon. But closer study reveals a few important differences. Basically, the features of Mercury's terrain can be divided into six categories: *craters*, *rays*, mountains, *basins*, *plains*, and *scarps*.

CRATERS, MOUNTAINS, AND RAYS

Craters are the most common feature found on Mercury. *Mariner 10* captured photos of millions of craters, ranging from a few hundred feet to 800 miles (1,290 km) in diameter.

Halley's Comet, seen in 1986. Scientists
think that Mercury's craters were formed
when flying objects like this one smashed
into the planet's surface.

Craters were formed when Mercury was bombarded by flying objects — such as meteoroids, asteroids, and perhaps *comets*. When our solar system was created billions of years ago these objects were constantly whizzing about. Each time one crashed into a planet's surface, it left a giant scar.

The craters are ten times bigger than the objects that formed them. They are surrounded by smaller holes called "secondary impact craters." Apparently, the flying objects exploded on impact and sent smaller fragments traveling for thousands of miles, creating their own minicraters.

Other craters sprayed particles of dust that formed a pattern like bicycle spokes. These are called rays. The impact of the projectiles also caused mountains to form in the middle of some of Mercury's larger craters. These mountains were created by the inrush of material that forced some of it to peak in the crater's center.

Scientists figure that most of Mercury's craters, especially the larger ones, were formed more than 4 billion years ago. Many small craters, however, have been created since then. It's possible that, as you're reading

An artist's conception of a flying object striking
Mercury's surface, forming a new crater, which
is surrounded by many older ones.

this, a meteoroid is crashing onto Mercury's surface.

If projectiles were once flying about the solar system, why isn't Earth also pockmarked with craters? Well, if Earth were without an atmosphere, like Mercury and the moon, and therefore had no winds, weather, or surface water, it too would be covered with craters today. Because Mercury has very little atmosphere, there have been very few changes on its surface and virtually all craters have remained. The meteoroids that made it through to Earth *did* create some craters, but eventually they were eroded away by wind, water, and geological forces. There are, however, still examples of craters on Earth, including one nearly 1 mile (1.6 km) across formed some 50,000 years ago in northern Arizona.

BASINS

The largest craters are called basins. The biggest of these jumbo craters is located near one of Mercury's hottest points, and so it is named the Caloris Basin, after the Latin word for *heat* (from which we get our English word

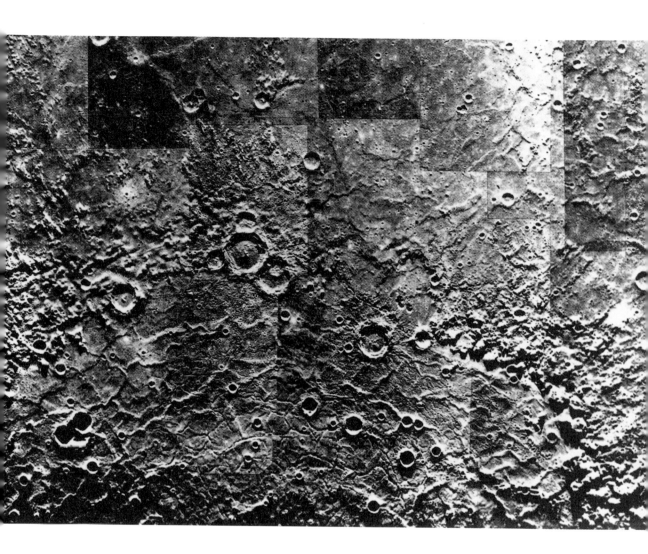

The mountains on the bottom of this photo form the edge of the Caloris Basin, one of the largest craters in the solar system. Even the smaller secondary craters are as big as 12 miles (20 km) in diameter.

calorie, which actually refers to a measurement of heat).

The Caloris Basin is *enormous* — one of the largest craters found anywhere in our solar system. With a diameter of about 800 miles (1,290 km), it could swallow up the state of Texas. Its secondary craters are themselves as large as 12 miles (20 km) in diameter. The basin is surrounded by a ring of mountains, making it nearly 1 mile (1.6 km) deep from floor to mountaintop.

The impact that created the Caloris Basin must have been devastating. In fact, it was so powerful that shock waves rippled through Mercury, shaking and tearing the ground on the exact opposite side (called the *antipodal* point) of the planet. This area is now an odd, lumpy region of hills and valleys. Scientists analyzing the *Mariner 10* data gave the area a nickname: "the weird terrain."

PLAINS

Plains (also called *planitia*) are the flat, broad, and smooth (except for an occasional wrinkle or small crater) areas between craters. They make up about 60 percent of Mercury's surface.

The plains aren't terribly exciting to look at, but they provide important clues about Mercury's past. What they suggest is that billions of years ago, when the planet was first forming, it was extremely hot — so hot that it melted from the inside. The heat caused the planet to expand (most objects expand when they are heated). This, in turn, cracked Mercury's thin shell, and enormous amounts of molten lava erupted from long cracks in the ground. When the lava pools cooled and hardened, they formed the smooth plains.

Scientists are not positive that this volcanic theory is correct. But until they can bring back and examine rock samples, this is their best guess.

SCARPS

We said earlier that most of Mercury's landscape resembles Earth's moon. *Scarps* are the big exception. In fact, no other planet displays such geological oddities, at least to such an extent.

Scarps are basically long, rounded cliffs. They stand from 1,000 feet (300 m) to almost 2 miles (3.2 km) high, and run from 10 to more

At the very top of this photo (taken by Mariner 10),
you can see one of Mercury's major scarps.
It extends southward for hundreds of miles.

than 300 miles (16 to 480 km) long. Sometimes they seem to wander aimlessly; other times they cut across the surface in almost perfectly parallel lines.

Like plains, these giant cliffs also stem from Mercury's birth. When the planet grew hot it expanded; when the planet cooled it began to contract. This shrinking caused huge portions of the surface to drop below an adjoining area. The result was scarps.

WHAT'S IN A NAME?

Having identified all of Mercury's surface features, scientists were left with one final (and fun) task: giving them names.

There were so many different features to name, the International Astronomical Union voted to divide them into categories. Craters, they decided, would be named for artists, writers, and musicians: Shakespeare, Tolstoy, Dostoevsky, and Beethoven were some of the people so honored. Valleys were given the names of radio observatories (such as Arecibo), and scarps the names of ships that once explored Earth (such as *Discovery*). Finally, plains were given the names used for

Astronomers named one of Mercury's plains for Odin, the Scandinavian father of the gods. Other plains were given the names used for Mercury in various ancient cultures.

Mercury in many ancient cultures (such as Odin). There are a few exceptions, most notably the Caloris Basin.

ICE FIELDS

Almost everything scientists know about Mercury's surface, they know from *Mariner 10*. In 1991, however, scientists were shocked and surprised by something new. Using radar, they learned that parts of Mercury — the closest planet to the sun — might be covered by huge sheets of ice!

The radar experiments made images of the side of Mercury not photographed by *Mariner 10*. Included were images of the north pole, where temperatures drop as low as –279° F (–171° C). Here scientists found a reflective surface — possibly ice — covering nearly 150 square miles (390 sq km).

The scientists were excited because they believed Earth's moon, which has somewhat similar conditions to Mercury, might also have hidden sheets of ice. If so, future lunar explorers could rely on this frozen water and not have to bring supplies of their own.

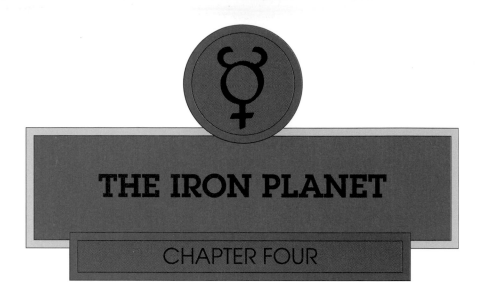

THE IRON PLANET

Although we are naturally most interested in surfaces, many of the things that make Mercury such an interesting planet are happening *inside*, way below the surface. Of course it's difficult for scientists working millions of miles away to know everything about a planet's insides. But by using *Mariner 10*'s experiments as well as earthbound calculations, they have pieced together a picture of Mercury's *core*. And it's quite an unusual picture. The other planets closest to the sun — Venus, Earth, and Mars — are mostly made of rock. The outer planets are primarily composed of gas and ice. Mercury, however, is almost 70 percent iron!

Venus, Mercury's closest neighbor, is mostly
made of rock. Mercury, however, is nearly 70 percent
iron, making it unusual among the inner planets.

DENSITY

Although Mercury is one of the smallest planets, it is second only to Earth in *density*, or the compactness of its materials. In fact, if you're talking about *uncompressed* density (density figured without the squeezing effects of gravity), Mercury is number one in the solar system. Because of this high density, it is almost certain that Mercury is made up of a large amount of iron. Scientists estimate that the planet is nearly 70 percent iron (by weight). This is twice as much iron as any other planet in our solar system. Earth is only about 35 percent iron.

The question is, where is all this iron found? It could be evenly distributed throughout the planet. Scientists think, however, that, like Earth, Mercury has a solid iron core — a huge metallic ball at the very center of the planet. This core is thought to be more than 2,200 miles (3,540 km) in diameter. That's larger than Earth's moon! It takes up nearly three-quarters of the planet's diameter. Surrounding the core is a layer of rock called the *mantle*. At the surface there is another thin layer of rock called the *crust*.

Many planets have iron. Mercury is unusual in having virtually all its iron in one place, the core. The reason for this, again, goes back to the story of the planet's formation. At one point, billions of years ago, the iron was evenly distributed, mixed in with the rock. But in the early days, the planet was so hot that it melted. The iron, which was heavier, separated from the rock and sank toward the center.

Scientists think the metallic core is still in a melted state, but they're not sure how or why. Maybe there is a source of heat somewhere in Mercury's interior. Or maybe the iron is mixed with an element, such as sulfur, that melts at low temperatures.

THE BIG BANG

Why does Mercury, compared to the other planets, have so much iron and so little rock? One theory is that the planets and moons of our solar system were formed from an enormous cloud of gas and dust called the solar nebula. The planets started as small rocks and slowly accumulated dust until they reached their present size. Mercury was closest to the sun, where the dust particles were high in iron and other elements that were not evaporated by the intense heat.

A drawing of the Big Bang, the explosive event that
created our solar system. Some scientists think
Mercury got its metallic core because it was so close
to the red-hot center pictured here.

More recently, astronomers have come up with a more violent theory. Four or five billion years ago, *after* the planets and other objects had formed from the solar nebula, these enormous orbs (spherical bodies) started zooming around, leaving their orbits and crossing the paths of other enormous orbs. Eventually, some of the planets collided head on — at speeds of up to 50,000 miles (80,000 km) per hour!

Earth and Venus were big enough to survive the collisions, but a little planet like Mercury was in constant danger of being blown to smithereens. In fact, the theory goes, one collision was harsh enough to knock Mercury for a loop. It survived, but most of its rocky mantle was blasted off and sent flying into space, leaving the metal core.

MAGNETIC FIELD

When *Mariner 10* sailed past Mercury, scientists were surprised to find the presence of magnetic forces, called a *magnetic field*. (Earth's magnetic field is what makes compasses always point in a general north-south direction.) Mercury's field is not very strong, less than 1 percent as strong as Earth's. But Mars and Venus have almost no magnetic fields, and the same was expected from Mercury. Scientists think you can't have a magnetic field without a molten metallic core, so this finding might be evidence that Mercury's core is at least partly melted.

A DAY ON MERCURY

CHAPTER FIVE

Even with today's technology, it is impossible to send human beings to Mercury. But imagine that you are a member of the first flight crew to visit the sun's closest neighbor. What will it look like? Will it be hot or cold? Can you run and jump? Is there oxygen to breathe?

ORBIT

First, just how long is a day? If a day is the time that passes from one sunrise to the next, one day on Mercury lasts two Earth years!

Mercury spins once on its axis every 58.6 Earth days. (Our planet rotates once every 24 hours; that's one Earth day.) It takes nearly 88

The solar system; Mercury is the tiny dot closest to the sun. Compared to the paths of the other planets, Mercury has the smallest orbit.

Earth days to finish one trip around the sun. Therefore, Mercury rotates three times as it orbits the sun twice. This three-to-two ratio is unique in our solar system.

Compared to the other planets, Mercury rotates on its axis at a very slow rate. On the other hand, it is the fastest planet when it comes to orbiting the sun. This odd combination makes for a very, very long day.

Imagine that you're standing still on Mercury's surface at sunrise. After half an orbit around the sun (or 44 Earth days) the planet has made three-quarters of a turn; it is noon. One complete orbit (88 Earth days) and Mercury has rotated three times, or gone through three more sunrises.

THE SUN AND STARS

Mercury's odd orbit and rotation produce other bizarre effects as well. If you were standing on the surface, looking at the eastern horizon, the sun would rise, stop, and then, seeming to change its mind, set! Then it would rise again to start the long day. At another point on Mercury's surface you might see the exact opposite event — the sun would set, rise back up, and then set again in the same place.

Why? Mercury changes speed during its orbit around the sun. When it is close to the sun it travels much faster. In fact, at this point near the sun, it orbits faster than it rotates. When it is far from the sun, it rotates faster than it orbits. This makes it appear that the sun is moving in the opposite direction. It actually seems to travel backward in the sky!

One other thing you would notice: the sun would look *huge*. From Mercury's surface it would appear three times bigger than it does from Earth. Because Mercury has no air, however, its sky is black even when the sun is up. Therefore you could see the brightest stars in the daytime, if you could shield your eyes from the intense glare of the sun and its brilliant light reflected off Mercury's landscape.

GRAVITY

Gravity is an unseen force that pulls objects toward a planet. Without it you could jump and never return to Earth. A ball tossed into the air would travel forever in space.

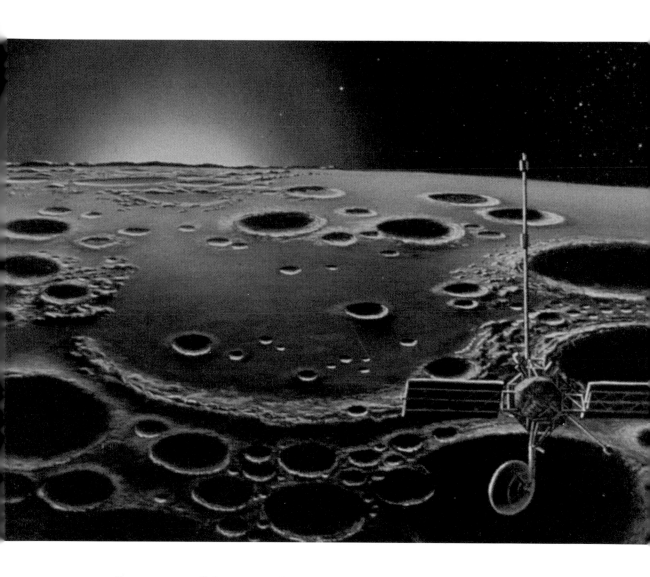

Because Mercury is so close to the sun, the sun appears three times bigger than it does from Earth. (Mariner 10 is in the foreground.)

As a rule, the smaller the planet, the weaker its gravity. But density is also a factor. By comparison, Mercury's gravitational pull is about one-third as strong as Earth's. If you weigh 100 pounds (45 kg) on Earth, you would weigh only 38 pounds (17 kg) on Mercury's surface.

ATMOSPHERE

When traveling to Mercury, don't forget your space suit. Among the gases surrounding Mercury that make up the planet's very thin *atmosphere*, there is not nearly enough oxygen, the gas that people need to breathe.

Astronomers have found that Mercury's atmosphere is very thin, only one-trillionth as dense as Earth's atmosphere. *Mariner 10* experiments told us that it is made up mostly of hydrogen and helium, the same light gases that cause balloons to float. The helium molecules probably come from the sun. As they blow by Mercury, they are trapped by the planet's gravitational field, but the field is too weak to hold them. So after a brief moment in Mercury's atmosphere, they escape into space.

In 1985, scientists determined that sodium is actually the most common element in

Mercury's atmosphere. (The instruments on *Mariner 10* were not sensitive to sodium.) The origin of this sodium is a mystery. It may come from inside Mercury or from tiny meteorites that hit the planet's surface and vaporize.

TEMPERATURE

You will need your space suit to protect you from the intense heat or cold, depending on where you're standing. Because Mercury is the closest planet to the sun, you might expect it to be the hottest planet. Actually, Mercury's neighbor Venus, which is farther from the sun, can be more than 100° F (38° C) hotter. The clouds that surround Venus trap the heat from the sun (much as do the panes of glass in a greenhouse). Mercury has no clouds, so much of its heat escapes into space. Still, Mercury gets very hot. At its most broiling, it can reach 800° F (420° C). By comparison, the normal oven temperature is about 350° F (175° C). Paper catches fire at 451° F (231° C).

Mercury also gets very cold on the night side, reaching lows of –279° F (–171° C), much, much colder than the Earth's North Pole. No other planet has such an extreme range of

temperatures. Why? Mercury rotates so slowly that one side takes in the sunlight for six Earth weeks, giving it lots of time to heat up. An equally long night gives the other side plenty of time to cool off, too. Also, because the planet has no atmosphere to insulate it, heat soaked up by the surface during the day leaks away into space after sunset.

As you're making your way across the surface of Mercury, beware of the "hot poles"! These are two extremely hot spots, on opposite sides of the equator, that face the sun when Mercury passes closest to that fiery orb. The "hot poles" are several hundred degrees warmer than surrounding regions, and their heat penetrates deep below the surface.

Mercury's day and night sides as photographed by Mariner 10. The difference in temperature between the two sides can be greater than one thousand degrees!

THE FUTURE

CHAPTER SIX

Until a couple of decades ago, we knew little about the nature of Mercury. *Mariner 10* increased our understanding a thousand-fold. Still, Mercury, hiding in the intense glare of the sun, remains a mystery.

Mars and Venus, our nearest neighbors, have each been inspected by a dozen or so probes. Faraway Jupiter and Saturn have had several visitors (of the nonhuman variety). And, of course, Earth's moon has actually been visited by humans. But Mercury has been visited only three times (by the same spacecraft).

Understandably, astronomers who specialize in Mercury have a great many questions.

Mariner 10 was the first — and only — spacecraft to explore Mercury. Scientists would like to send another probe to answer their many questions about this mysterious planet.

There is, for example, the case of the core, the huge iron ball at the planet's center. Why does Mercury have so much iron? Was it always that way, or did a collision with a runaway object knock much of its rock off?

Then there's the matter of the magnetic field. Scientists always thought such a field was created by both a hot, liquid core and a fast rotation that would set the core spinning. Mercury rotates very slowly; yet it has a magnetic field. Why? The answer may sharpen our understanding of the Earth's magnetic field, which helps to protect us from dangerous radiation from outer space.

Many more questions remain. Why does Mercury have so many craters and basins? Were they formed by comets and meteoroids, or made during the birth of the solar system by leftover pieces of planets? And why is Mercury so small? Was it once a moon of Venus that was pushed out of its orbit by a collision?

Only another Mercury orbiter, like *Mariner 10*, could answer these questions. It could tell us more about Mercury's atmosphere. It could also photograph the 55 percent of the planet's surface that was missed by *Mariner 10*. Who knows what is lurking on this other side — different surface features, perhaps, such as giant volcanoes.

Eventually, to unravel the mystery of the core, scientists will need to get a surface sample — a rock or a dirt sample. This can be accomplished only by a spacecraft landing on Mercury and launching a robot rover to comb the planet collecting rock samples.

It would be expensive, but worth the trip. Answering these questions will teach us not only about Mercury but also about the entire solar system and how it was formed. And that, in turn, will teach us more about Earth, our home planet, and what we can do to protect it.

Unfortunately, NASA (the National Aeronautics and Space Administration) has no plans to return to Mercury in this century. Russian scientists are discussing a Mercury probe, but it would not blast off until 2002 or 2003. It looks as if mysterious Mercury, the planet that has frustrated astronomers for centuries, will remain elusive for at least a few more years.

FACT SHEET ON MERCURY

Symbol for Mercury — ☿

Position — Mercury is the closest planet to the sun. Within the solar system it is between the sun and Venus.

Rotation period — 58.646 Earth days

Length of year — 88 Earth days

Diameter — 3,031 miles (4,880 km)

Distance from the sun (depending on location in orbit) — least: 28,600,000 miles (46,046,000 km); greatest: 43,400,000 miles (69,874,000 km)

Distance from Earth (depending on orbit) — least: 57,000,000 miles (91,770,000 km); greatest: 136,000,000 miles (218,896,000 km)

Temperature — ranges from 801° F (423° C) to –279° F (–171° C)

GLOSSARY

Antipodal points — points on exact opposite sides of a planet

Asteroids — small, planetlike bodies

Astronomer — a scientist who studies the universe beyond the Earth

Atmosphere — the various gases that surround some planets

Axis — the imaginary line through a planet's center, around which it rotates

Basin — an especially large crater

Comet — a flying object made of ice, gas, and dust

Core — the innermost part of a planet

Crater — a bowl-shaped hole on a planet's surface, caused by the impact of a meteoroid

Crust — the rocky, outermost layer of a planet

Density — the compactness of materials

Gravitational field — the area around a planet in which an unseen force (gravity) pulls objects toward the planet's center

Magnetic field — the area around a planet in which a compass needle points to the magnetic north pole

Mantle — the middle layer of a planet, between its core and crust

Meteoroid — a flying body made of stone or metal

Orbit — the curved path of an object circling another object

Phases — the parts of a planet's surface that are lit by the sun and therefore visible on Earth

Plains — broad, smooth areas between craters

Probe — an unmanned spacecraft sent to study a planet or heavenly body

Radar — a method of bouncing radio waves off far-away objects to determine their size, shape, speed, and other characteristics (short for radio detecting and ranging)

Rays — bright lines, formed by flying dust particles, that radiate out from a crater in a bicycle-spoke pattern

Scarps — long, tall, rounded cliffs that cut across a planet's surface for hundreds of miles

FOR FURTHER READING

Asimov, Isaac. *Mercury, The Quick Planet.* Milwaukee: Gareth Stevens, 1989.

Chapman, Clark R. *The Inner Planets.* New York: Charles Scribner's Sons, 1977.

Fradin, Dennis B. *Mercury.* Chicago: Childrens Press, 1990.

Malin, Stuart. *The Greenwich Guide to the Planets.* Cambridge, England: Cambridge University Press, 1989.

Murray, Bruce C. *Flight to Mercury.* New York: Columbia University Press, 1977.

Ryan, Peter. *Solar System.* New York: Viking, 1978.

Strom, Robert G. *Mercury: The Elusive Planet.* Washington, D.C.: Smithsonian Institution Press, 1987.

Vogt, Gregory. *Mars and the Inner Planets.* New York: Franklin Watts, 1982.

INDEX

ABOUT THE AUTHOR

Robert Daily received a B.A. in English literature from Carleton College and a master's
degree in English literature, from the University
of Chicago. He is a magazine writer for both
adults and children and is also the author of
Earth in the First Book series. He lives with his
wife, Janet, in Chicago.